HEADWATERS

 Poems

Also by ELLEN BRYANT VOIGT

Poetry

Claiming Kin

The Forces of Plenty

The Lotus Flowers

Two Trees

Kyrie

Shadow of Heaven

Messenger: New and Selected Poems, 1976–2006

Prose

The Flexible Lyric

The Art of Syntax: Rhythm of Speech, Rhythm of Song

HEADWATERS

 Poems

Ellen Bryant Voigt

W. W. Norton & Company

New York • London

Copyright © 2013 by Ellen Bryant Voigt

For information about permission to reproduce selections from this book,
write to Permissions, W. W. Norton & Company, Inc.,
500 Fifth Avenue, New York, NY 10110

For information about special discounts for bulk purchases, please contact
W. W. Norton Special Sales at specialsales@wwnorton.com or 800-233-4830

Manufacturing by Courier Westford
Production manager: Louise Mattarelliano

Library of Congress Cataloging-in-Publication Data

Voigt, Ellen Bryant, date.
[Poems. Selections]
Headwaters : poems / Ellen Bryant Voigt. — First edition.
    pages ; cm.
ISBN 978-0-393-08320-0 (hardcover)
I. Title.
PS3572.O34H43 2013
811'.54—dc23
            2013009650

W. W. Norton & Company, Inc.
500 Fifth Avenue, New York, N.Y. 10110
www.wwnorton.com

W. W. Norton & Company Ltd.
Castle House, 75/76 Wells Street, London W1T 3QT

1 2 3 4 5 6 7 8 9 0

CONTENTS

ACKNOWLEDGMENTS

Thanks to the editors who first published these poems:

The American Poetry Review: Birch, Garter Snake, Hound, Lament, Milkmaid, Moles, Noble Dog, Oak, Spring, Stones

The American Scholar: Headwaters, Larch, My Mother, Sleep

The Atlantic: Fox, Hog-Nosed Skunk, Yearling

Blackbird: Lost Boy

The Cortland Review: Maestro

Granta: Geese

The New Yorker: Bear, Chameleon, Cow, Owl, Roof, Storm

The New York Times: Privet Hedge

HEADWATERS

 Poems

HEADWATERS

I made a large mistake I left my house I went into the world it was not
the most perilous hostile part but I couldn't tell among the people there

who needed what no tracks in the snow no boot pointed toward me or away
no snow as in my dooryard only the many currents of self-doubt I clung

to my own life raft I had room on it for only me you're not surprised
it grew smaller and smaller or maybe I grew larger and heavier

but don't you think I'm doing better in this regard I try to do better

PRIVET HEDGE

first frail green in the northeast the forest around us no longer
a postcard of Christmas snow clotting the spruce or worse
fall's technicolor beeches sumac sugar maple death
even the death of vegetation should never be
so beautiful it is unseemly I prefer the cusps
they focus the mind
                              which otherwise stays
distracted knowing things when my friend said
knowledge does nothing for him I felt at once superior
and chastised I'd just deduced the five new birds in my yard
woodpecker size and stripes and red blaze but feeding on the ground
five yellow-shafted flickers can the soul be known by its song who hears it
what keeps it aloft what keeps it whole what helps it survive habitual
pride greed wrath sloth lust a list compiled by a parent always
needing something to forgive you for I meant

to ask the nuns to straighten this out for me
while I was among them in Minnesota their earlier spring
but I couldn't guess which ones they are they dress
like everyone else no veils no starched white
no kneeling boards I was left on my own
to study the graveyard behind the privet hedge

their markers all alike as on a battlefield immense and calm

beneath an open midwestern sky nothing between

the pilgrim and the scoured horizon

STONES

birds not so much the ducks and geese okay not horses cows pigs
she'd lived in the city all her life some cats and dogs okay as part

of someone else's narrative the posted photographs are someone's
pets the figurines less figurative than graceful to behold the same

with carved giraffes and camels no reptiles no amphibians nothing
from the sea although she loved the sea her passion was for stones

I don't know why the parquet floor never buckled and caved collapsed
into the rooms below her rooms all the horizontal surfaces were covered

with stones the bureau the cupboards the closets were full of the precious
stones she wore at her throat her ears her fingers her wrists the inlaid

tables held ceramic bowls of polished stones the antique desk a basket
of stones a bushel of stones on the floor on the windowsills more stones

each one unique each one a narrative the étagère held up to the light stones
hewn from the source and hauled up here still jagged refracting every

shade of amethyst her birthstone like my mother's crystals shimmering
as if alive rescued from the field the cliff the shore the riverbed I found

a single cufflink by her bed a tiny diamond set in silver did her father
sift out at his flour mill the dangerous stones I stretched out beside her

in her bad time thinking to help her sleep I held her hand her fingers wore
a few of her favorite rings the two of us lay entirely still atop the quilt

a stiff sarcophagus she didn't sleep her mind was an etched plate
from which she drew off print after print the framed prints on the walls

were all interiors our talk had always been a stone kicked down a hill
no purpose no destination her father her mother my mother my dogs

she never said she was leaving me in charge she wasn't my mother why
put me in charge I put the jewels on other throats and wrists I threw away

the bushels of cosmetics and perfume her chosen armaments
against the world who loved the world I sold the breakfront

cabinet full of cut-glass bowls and blown glass figurines but who
will save the living stones she loved I have so many already

in my yard half-in half-out of the earth immovable
she'd seen my yard she'd seen those heavy stones

OAK

not to board the bus but wait for the last bell
like those who live in town shuffling ahead of her the clumps
drift apart drift back shifting boys in a cluster now a boy and a girl
a dance a recess game as each is subtracted one by one into the houses
she passes the windows half-lidded by half-drawn shades
or framed by curtains and sash she likes

                                              walking alone
along the verge of the lawns no fence no field the leaves
drifting out from under the oaks while in the woods
they would only settle and rot she likes the way a passing car
releases them across the grid of the sidewalk a solid math
for a solitary girl the small steps into the larger
world of strangers wholly indifferent houses cars rust-colored dog
she passes the hardware grocery pharmacy beauty salon every Thursday
you've noticed such a child content to be invisible
scuffing the leaves

                           toward the bungalow the hushed backroom
where someone is propped in the high bed her webbed face
her halo of hair past humankind and all its suffering
past seeing now past death too old for death
and waiting for this girl

                                 who thumbs the latch

who lifts the lid of the black box lifts from red felt those silver pieces
fits them together the trick is to breathe across and not
into the small round hole as her arched fingers hover
over the other open holes each finger knows its task she's fixed
to one purpose *Joyful Joyful We Adore Thee*

dark out in the street the wind ruffling oak leaves the dark
window lit by the silver flute the white ghost hair the brighter
lights is it her mother come to drive her home

MY MOTHER

my mother my mother my mother she
could do anything so she did everything the world
was an unplowed field a dress to be hemmed a scraped knee it needed
a casserole it needed another alto in the choir her motto was apply yourself
the secret of life was spreading your gifts why hide your light
under a bushel you might

forget it there in the dark times the lonely times
the sun gone down on her resolve she slept a little first
so she'd be fresh she put on a little lipstick drawing on her smile
she pulled that hair up off her face she pulled her stockings on she stepped
into her pumps she took up her matching purse already
packed with everything they all would learn
they would be nice they would

apologize they would be grateful whenever
they had forgotten what to pack she never did
she had a spare she kissed your cheek she wiped the mark
away with her own spit she marched you out again unless you were
that awful sort of stubborn broody child who more and more
I was who once had been so sweet so mild staying put
where she put me what happened

must have been the bushel I was hiding in

the sun gone down on her resolve she slept a little first

so she'd be fresh she pulled her stockings on she'd packed

the words for my every lack she had a little lipstick on her teeth the mark

on my cheek would not rub off she gave the fluids from her mouth

to it she gave the tissues in her ample purse to it I never did

apologize I let my sister succor those in need and suffer

the little children my mother

knew we are self-canceling she gave herself

a lifetime C an average grade from then on out she kept

the lights on day and night a garden needs the light the sun

could not be counted on she slept a little day and night she didn't need

her stockings or her purse she watered she weeded she fertilized she stood

in front the tallest stalk keeping the deer the birds all

the world's idle shameless thieves away

OWL

the sign for making the most of what you have
on the human hand is a thumb at full right angle to the palm
for the owl it's two talons forward two back a flexible foot
that crushes the prey and lifts it to the beak to the eyes
which are legally blind this is why the owl

hunts in the dark in the dusk when nothing is clearly seen
and why the owl's eyes are fixed facing ahead to better focus
so its whole face swivels in each direction like the turret on a tank
the round plates of feathers surrounding the eyes collect the least sound
when it turns the owl is computing by geometry the exact

location of the mouse or snake or songbird
that moves imperceptibly in its nest toward which the owl
sets out from the hole in the tree the burrow the eave of the barn
and crosses the field in utter silence wing-feathers overlapped
to make no sound poor mouse poor rabbit
                                        last night
from the porch obbligato to the brook and the snuffling deer
intent on the gnarled worm-bitten apples we leave on the tree
I heard what must have been a Barred Owl or a Barn Owl
or a Lesser Horned Owl close by not deep in the woods
what I heard was less a call than a cry

a fragment repeating repeating a kind of shudder
which may be why the country people I come from
thought an owl was prescient ill-omen meant to unspool
the threads they'd gathered and wound I was a grown woman
when my father took the key from under the eave

and unlocked the door to the darkened house he had grown up in
and stepped across the threshold and said as he entered the empty room
hello Miss Sally as though his stepmother dead for weeks
were still in her usual chair
                    in the Medicine Wheel
the emblem for wisdom is the same for gratitude at dusk at dark
the farsighted owl strikes in utter silence when we hear it
from the tree or the barn what it announces
is already finished

MILKMAID

white froth overnight on bare ground brown leaves
no yellow bus on the snow-slicked road so I could help my father
deliver the mail his other job begin at six finish at two then farm

my part was laboring through the drifts
toward the red flag the widow's flag meant
dried-apple pies fried pockets of fruit to sweeten

his usual bitter thermos his usual two sandwiches
one butter sliced in a slab the peasant's cheese one meat
maybe headcheese the leftover parts of pig snowdays

I wore his fishing boots rolled at my waist
I waded to the metal box put something in took something out
I still believe getting the mail is the best part of the day my beloved

disagrees he says he has enough bad news but what about finding
among the trash a piece of smooth beach glass today a postcard
a milkmaid's royal blue emphatic apron

not dulled by many washings not stained by milk or mud the blue
Vermeer's ennoblement he lets her pour a pure white stream
from the lip of the pitcher into the earthbrown bowl

what's rich has been set aside for butter or cheese
what's left enough to soften the week's stale bread a peasant's
Sunday supper Milk Soup my father's favorite

YEARLING

Thanksgiving Day was the day they slaughtered the hog the carcass
hoisted by its heels from the oak the planks across sawhorses holding
the hams the buckets catching the blood the shanks the organ meats
the chunks of white fat for biscuits the feet sunk in brine as the yard-dogs
whined for the leathery ear and my grandmother napped
with the baby always a baby needing a nap

                                        my neighbor
at ninety-six claims she's never had a nap she has no use for dogs
she used to spend Thanksgiving in the woods getting her deer
and strung it up outside the shed where now droops
head down rack down her son's deer her knives
stay sharp one year her son brought by

not venison a yearling bear glossy and black
dressed out there wasn't much underneath its thick coat
a scrawny frame the paws so much like hands she said
when she looked through the window it startled her
hanging there the size of a child

COW

end of the day daylight subsiding into the trees lights coming on
in the milking barns as somewhere out in the yard some ants
are tucking in their aphids for the night behind
hydrangea leaves or in their stanchions underground
they have been bred for it the smaller brain

serving the larger brain the cows eat so we will eat we guarantee
digestion is the only work they do heads down tails up
they won't have sex they get some grain some salt
no catamounts no wolves we fertilize the fields
we put up bales of hay we give them names

but again this week one breached the fence the neighbors
stopped to shoo it back a girl held out a handful of grass
calling the cow as you would a dog no dice so what
if she recoiled to see me burst from the house with an ax
I held it by the blade I tapped with the handle where the steaks come from

like the one I serve my friend a water sign who likes to lurk
in the plural solitude of Zen retreat to calm his mind but when it's done
what he needs I think is something truly free of mind a slab of earth
by way of cow by way of fire the surface charred the juices
running pink and red on the white plate

FOX

rangy loping swiveling left then right I'm thinking
nonchalant but the doves flutter up to the roof of the barn the crickets
leap from the grass like fleas a fox is in my yard-o my yard-o
plenty of songs in my head

to sing to my child's child if she were here
she wakes in her wooden crib and sings to herself
odd happy child so like another child content in her pen
with a pot a metal straw a lid a hole in the lid a glass hat
for the hole a metal basket with smaller holes
one hole the size of the straw for hours

I made the pieces fit then took them apart
then made them fit when I got tired I lay me down my little head
against the flannel chicks and ducks then slept then woke then took
the puzzle up my mother had another child sick unto death
she needed me to fall in love with solitude I fell in love
it is my toy my happiness the child of my friends
is never ever left alone asleep awake
pushing her wooden blocks around the rug they cannot bear
her least distress their eyes stay on their sparrow poor happy child

last year I startled a fox crossing the road the tail
more rust than red the head cranked forward facing me
it stopped stock-still as if deciding whether to hurry forward
or turn back it had a yellow apple in its mouth
and the little ones chew on the bones-o

NOBLE DOG

behind our house down to the brook and the woods
beyond the groomed grass and flower beds what we see
are brook and woods and sometimes mild creatures of the field
we thought when we bathed in the claw-footed tub we could pretend
we stayed inside the natural world no shutters no shades at night

beside the mirror over the sink the windows darkened into mirrors
where my daughter at thirteen admired her tan her new body until she felt
or thought she felt something move outside in the yard and asked quietly
up the backstairs for us to come down here for just a minute please
come down here now we couldn't tell how much was fear

how much was shame we thought she needed us to be calm
we tried to be calm like the trooper we called who said without alarm
to the handsome noble dog where is he buddy where is he buddy
at which as if in a game of fetch the dog went straight around the house
to the one smell that didn't fit to the one smell that crossed the clipped grass

into the ditch beside the dirt road where the dog went too the dog
tracking the smell the trooper tracking the dog the dog
not barking or baying until the scent stopped
inside the culvert bearing the brook west under the road
a large metal pipe that amplified the dog's whimpers and moans

dog of righteousness dog of retribution

we heard it from our house where soon the shutters would go up
we sat in the kitchen the summer air soft as a damp rag we knew
this was a moment of consequence but we couldn't tell
whether the world had grown larger or smaller

MOLES

where is his hat where is his horse where is his harrier my beloved
is distraught he made this yard each blade each stem each stalk except
the mounds of fresh dirt like little graves it's moles that make the mounds
when they make holes they're worms with fur the cat

does not do moles she's stalking rooks and mice beloved
has scattered human hair across the sod it keeps the deer away
he has installed a high-pitched hum in the lily bed it keeps the dogs
out of the yard who might have otherwise unearthed a mole too bad

traps don't work the way they do for squirrels my father
used to thrust the hose into one hole and flood them out my beloved
does not care what my father did this greensward is his joy his job
my job was children food house the rest of what I did stayed underground

GARTER SNAKE

hibernaculum a hole in the earth

from which in spring the snakes ooze forth the males

much smaller than the female stretched out like a tree-limb

among the tulips not moving not rippling or flinching preoccupied

a film over her eyes along her body the smaller snakes

flex and extend they may be helping her shed or may be

roughhousing like little boys which is what I thought at the pond

when I saw three mallards jump another duck they stayed underwater

a very long time she never did resurface the female snake seems

oblivious sheathed in ribbons one of them shudders off

and shimmies toward the lilac hedge our friend

wants to show us he can catch a snake at the top of its spine

and reaches into the grass but even a garter snake

has teeth we see it flung then reinvented half erect

on its coils hissing or taking soundings with its tongue

swiveling its head to follow the enemy

that's us

GROUNDHOG

not unlike otters which we love frolicking
floating on their backs like truant boys unwrapping lunch
same sleek brown pelt some overtones of gray and rust
though groundhogs have no swimming hole and lunch
is rooted in the ground beneath short legs small feet
like a fat man's odd diminutive loafers not

frolicking but scurrying layers of fat his coat
gleams as though wet shines chestnut sable darker
head and muzzle lower into the grass a dark
triangular face like the hog-nosed skunk another delicate
nose and not a snout doesn't it matter what they're called I like swine

which are smart and prefer to be clean using their snouts
to push their excrement to the side of the pen
but they have hairy skin not fur his fur
shimmers and ripples he never uproots the mother plant his teeth
I think are blunt squared off like a sheep's if cornered does he
cower like sheep or bite like a sow with a litter is he ever

attacked he looks to me inedible he shares his acreage

with moles voles ravenous crows someone thought up
the names his other name is botched Algonquin but yes
he burrows beneath the barn where a farmer once

dried cordwood he scuttles there at speech cough laugh
at lawnmower swollen brook high wind he lifts his head
as Gandhi did small tilt to the side or stands erect
like a prairie dog or a circus dog but dogs don't waddle like Mao
with a tiny tail he seems asexual like Gandhi like Jesus if Jesus
came back would he be vegetarian also pinko freako homo

in Vermont natives scornful of greyhounds from the city
self-appoint themselves woodchucks unkempt hairy macho
who would shoot on sight an actual fatso shy mild marmot radiant
as the hog-nosed skunk in the squirrel trap both cleaner than sheep
fur fluffy like a girl's maybe he is a she it matters
what we're called words shape the thought don't say
rodent and ruin everything

HOG-NOSED SKUNK

because she's half blind and thus prefers
complete not partial darkness and because
she cannot raise her tail entirely over her back
in order to use her one weapon her one defense
when you come to the squirrel trap from behind
and cover with a blanket the wire box
although my beloved won't believe it
she just gives up she just gives up

HOUND

since thought is prayer if hard and true I thought that thought
could lead me to compassion for my fellow creatures
insects excluded contrary to the Buddha the wasps
might show a little compassion too I do include
the hound next door it moans all day all night
a loud slow lament a child can make itself sustain

to dramatize its misery this dog was once
the neighbors' child but now they have an actual child
he's been cast down to be a dog again chained outdoors heartsick
uncomprehending why can't he just buck up remember his roots his lot
not more special than any other
                              sad hound look up
at the fledglings' wide mouths look over here
at the cat teaching her litter how to hunt all sleek all black
they're interchangeable her many tits confirm no favorites
no first no last
                at least with only two
both can be a kind of favorite it's better than three
I ought to know my sister and I each had one parent to herself
like Tea for Two it wasn't hard to be the boy
until there came the actual boy he was nothing like my father
what does it mean to have flown from the same nest into the world

you're thinking one is best

                          one open mouth no first no last but isn't it
then the parents who compete no wonder the father of animals
wanders off the best is two all right one parent and one child
we've seen it work among the elephants

LOST BOY

who says we aren't primarily animals for instance

you recognize at once the smell of doom and keep away unless

you're drawn by pheromones like a soldier ant or for once you worry

about your soul he reeked of doom despised by those he loved one parent

missing one parent Pentecostal disgusted by the queer parts of him

he was himself disgusted self-despising snarling sick

unto death the chronic contagious sickness of our times

a righteous judgment was what he called it the rash

erupted over and over no meds no money no readiness

for help if there'd been help no self-defense unless you count

self-sabotage the wounds were old and ugly he kept them fresh he was quick

to take offense except from me and for what for merely a kindness

that brought me letters photos poems seeds saved from his yard roses

profuse on the cards for Mother's Day on valentines because I was a surrogate

it cost me nothing until he chose oblivion the news was no surprise his gift

was always making something out of nothing

MAESTRO

he smoked like a chimney we used to say unfiltered
Chesterfields the fragile horizontal column of ash
lengthening as he winced at the sour notes but plunged ahead
even when it splashed down onto the keyboard his long hands
showing the smaller hands how it was done the Chopin the Bach
or some reduction of the Nutcracker Suite whatever might be needed
in order to teach the young you also need

herculean belief in the possible and his had sugared off
into a pure elixir he must have sipped from
nights in his rented room in the widow's house I suppose
she cooked for him and always someone's mother had sent pie
everyone knew it wasn't us he loved
but he made his Chevrolet an open closet instruments and scores
and the book that conjured every known song
when there were two pianos the two of us

took turns the solo the orchestra imagine
the odds that he'd turn up in my life in time
to loosen the bony grip of Mrs. Law who kept
the ledger of your mistakes and whose breath could peel back bark
exactly as my older sister said when she leapt from the bench

and fled the lessons leaving me behind it didn't matter

whether I was worthy or unworthy he took me

everywhere in the Chevrolet he played

with flat fingers I do too

GEESE

there is no cure for temperament it's how
we recognize ourselves but sometimes within it
a narrowing imprisons or is opened such as when my mother
in her last illness snarled and spat and how this lifted my dour father
into a patient tenderness thereby astounding everyone
but mostly it hardens who we always were

if you've been let's say a glass-half-empty kind of girl
you wake to the chorus of geese overhead
forlorn for something has softened their nasal voices
their ugly aggression on the ground they're worse than chickens
but flying one leader falling back another moving up to pierce the wind
no one in charge or every one in charge in flight each limited goose
adjusts its part in the cluster just under the clouds
do they mean together to duplicate the cloud
like the pelicans on the pond rearranging their shadows
to fool the fish another collective that constantly recalibrates but fish
don't need to reinvent themselves the way geese do
when they negotiate the sky
                              on the fixed
unyielding ground there is no end to hierarchy
the flock the pack the family you know it's true if you're
a take-charge kind of girl I recommend

houseplants in the windows facing south
the cacti the cyclamen are blooming on the brink
of winter all it took was a little enforced deprivation
a little premature and structured dark

BIRCH

before it's too late I need to study the great religions time
is speeding up in the bad movie of my life months fly off
the calendar or the camera stays fixed on one tree
in leaf no leaves in leaf sunrise sunset
as the great Yiddish musical says

and then the *chuppah* the goblet smashed delirious dancers
parading the newlyweds in chairs like royalty but why
give up those beasts whose hooves leave valentines
for us in the muddy sty and why so much anxiety
regarding women ditto Mary's
beatific smile but I like distinctive hats on those in charge
and I know I need a little intercession spilt salt
flung over the shoulder a daily lineup facing east
though some of us have to pray in our personal tents
like snails
        a wedding in a garden
suits me fine the flowers left unsacrificed
it's Adam and Eve except that Adam had no mother
no one who worried about that missing rib now incarnate
wearing white like a young birch beside my boy who's grown
bewitched looking nowhere but at her I know that look

a Druid with his chosen tree he might as well

be on his knees he needs an altar something old something

once revered perhaps I could volunteer bring on the saw the guests

can bow their heads and count the rings the years

BEAR

pressed full-length against the screen unzipping it
for a better grip to help him help himself to the seed and the suet
slung high under the eave by the man
who has charged down from the bedroom onto the porch
in his white loincloth like David against Goliath
but only one good lung shouting swearing
and behind him the woman caught
at the lip of the lit kitchen
                              where was my sister
with her gun or would she be praying since she prays routinely
for a parking spot and there it is or would she be speechless for once
that this man so moderate so genial so unlike me
had put himself one body-length away from a full-grown bear
or would she be saying you my dear are the person who married him
which of course I did I did and I stood behind him
as he stood his ground on the ground that is our porch
                                                    you can see
the marks gouged by the famous claws on the wall inside new screen
now laced by a wire trellis on which nothing climbs
a vertical electric fence one of us thinks
the bear can hear it hum from the edge of the woods
watching us like a child sent to his room as we grill the salmon
we spiked with juniper berries the other one thinks

the plural pronoun is a dangerous fiction the source
of so much unexpected loneliness

CHAMELEON

beside myself in Texas the doctors asking my beloved
to give his pain a number one to ten his answer is always
two I tell them eight the holly bush in the yard is putting out new leaves
which makes its resident lizard bright green also light brown
along its slender spine a plausible twig
except the lining of its mouth is red as it puts away
in three quick bites some kind of fly and then at its throat
a rosy translucent sac swells and subsides maybe peristaltic
pushing its meal forward or maybe preening for a mate or maybe
residual from the blooming hibiscus shrub or maybe learned from frogs
that also live in a tree but singing is dangerous if you mean
to replicate vegetation
                              O exquisite creature
whose dull cousin back in Vermont the brown lizard
navigates our dooryard by alternating pairs of elbows like oars
determined and clumsy moving across the gravel yet moving forward
I see you do not move unless you need to eat you almost fool
the mockingbird nearby in a live oak tree flinging out another's song
which is me which which is me

LAMENT

absence neither sweet nor bitter
without the aftertaste of willfulness does it happen
as the dipper fixed in the northern sky turns
to lie on its side no longer facing east
where in late summer the bull rises with its bright red eye

or is it more like a rock in the swollen stream millennia
to bind its layered parts then battered cleaved
then one half tumbled away

idiopathic is what they say to say
no evident cause no trigger no blame except to blame
the way the world winds down winds up again shifting particles
as easily as pollen in the wind

stars stone lichen glued to the stone a human hand

and so one hand withdrawn from the other hand
what had been paired a left a right
                              every cell divides
in order to multiply it's where we began

SPRING

years of unearthing the rocks out of the field and soon enough
you've built a stone wall the longer the marriage

the less the need for trying to agree but we've agreed
what will happen at the end of it nothing

except the old immutable forms
like a shovel shared at the grave for texts

Ecclesiastes so the bereaved
can choose whether to believe

that death is a kind of hibernation this spring the groundhog
foraging in our yard was smaller thinner a strange

perpendicular crimp in its tail which proved
to the rational mind it was a different creature but look beloved

how by late summer it's fattened out how its coat now gleams how
when frightened it also hurries into the barn

SLEEP

another heavy frost what doesn't die or fly away
the groundhog for instance the bear is deep in sleep I'm thinking
a lot about sleep translation I'm not sleeping much
who used to be a champion of sleep
ex-champions are pathetic my inner parent says the world
is full of evil death cruelty degradation not sleeping
scores only 2 out of 10
                  but a moral sense
is exhausting I am exhausted a coma looks good to me
if only I could be sure there'd still be dreams it's what I miss the most
even in terrible dreams at least you feel what you feel not what
you're supposed to feel your house burns down so what
if you survived you rake the ashes sobbing
                        exhausted
from trying to not smoke I once asked for a simple errand
from my beloved who wanted me not to smoke he forgot unforgivable
I fled the house like an animal wounded enraged I was thinking
more clearly than I had ever thought my thought was why

prolong this life I flung myself into the car I drove like a fiend
to the nearest store I asked unthinking for unfiltered Luckies oh
brand of my girlhood I paid the price I took my prize to the car I slit
the cellophane I tapped out one perfect white cylinder I brought to my face

the smell of the barns the fires cooking it golden brown smell of my father

my uncles my grandfather's tin of loose tobacco his packet of delicate paper

the deliberate way he rolled and licked and tapped and lit and drew in

and relished it the smell of the wild girls behind the gym the boys

in pickup trucks I sat in my car as the other cars crept by

I looked like a pervert it was perverse

a Lucky under my nose

I drove myself home

I threw away the pack which was unwise the gods

don't notice whining they notice the brief bright flares of human will

they lean from their couches yes more fear and dread for that one

yes let's turn the suffering up a notch let's watch her

strike the match I strike it now when I wake

in the dark I light that little fire

LARCH

short-sleeves in Vermont late November the leaves long gone
only evergreens the white birch bark and our feral black cat
not sheltering prowling improbably in her thickened coat
one more free-range lunch one more of her nine lives
put back into reserve unlike the year's fresh deaths

as for me I keep my votive candles burning as the larches burned
on the hillside their needles yellow deciduous like the leaves
and now sloughed in the yard beneath the small larch
bent double cascading like a willow weeping is the proper name for it
also for the cherry tree in the yard of the house where my parents' friend
shot an intruder it was his wife their tree

might as well be here with all my other lost trees childhood mimosas
magnolias the willow oak blown down in a storm surviving in my head
beside the friend the murdered wife the subsequent wife
my parents too and now Peter with his lazy eye and glamorous
doom-ridden Rynn and Carol who had her own reprieves

who used them up I confess the weather matters more and more to me
diurnal is a lovely word another is circadian

ROOF

after a week of daily heavy snow I want to praise my roof first
the acute angle at which it descends from the ridgepole
and second that it is black the color absorbing
all the other colors so that even now as arctic air
blows in from the plains my roof burns off from underneath
the dazzling snow dense layers of particles which are tiny
specks of trash sheathed in wet cloud what chance
do they have against my roof even at night
the snowpack over my head breaks apart and slides on its own melting
down from the eaves as though my roof had shrugged I hear snow
thump to the ground a cleansing sound the secret of my roof
is standing seams the raised ridges
bonding the separate panels to one another an old
wound that has healed no lapped shingles catching the wind
no icejam at the eaves no sending my beloved out with an ax
no roof caved in from the weight of snow as happened in 1924 only
another thump as a slab of snow lets loose leaving my roof
gleaming in the wet residue it takes what it needs
from the lifesource and sheds the rest a useful
example if I were starting over

STORM

one minute a slender pine indistinguishable from the others
the next its trunk horizontal still green the jagged stump
a nest for the flickers
                              one minute high wind and rain the skies
lit up the next a few bright winking stars the lashing of the brook

one minute an exaltation in the apple trees the shadblow trees
the next white trash on the ground new birds
or the same birds crowding the feeder
one minute the children were sleeping in their beds

you got sick you got well you got sick

the lilac bush we planted is a tree the cat creeps past
with something in her mouth she's hurrying down to where

the culvert overflowed one minute bright yellow
marsh marigolds springing up the next
the farmer sweeps them into his bales of hay